Hollywood DOGS

by Meish Goldish

Consultant: Thomas Leitch
University of Delaware

BEARPORT
PUBLISHING

New York, New York

Credits

Cover and Title Page, © Showbiz Ireland/Getty Images; Cover (RT), © Buena Vista Pictures/ Everett Collection; Cover (RM), © Universal/Everett Collection; Cover (RB), © Buena Vista Pictures/Everett Collection; 3, © Buena Vista Pictures/Everett Collection; 4, Courtesy Everett Collection; 5, Courtesy Everett Collection; 6, Courtesy Everett Collection; 7, © MGM/Photofest; 8, © Bettmann/Corbis; 9, © Bettmann/Corbis; 10, Courtesy Everett Collection; 11, Courtesy Everett Collection; 12, Courtesy Everett Collection; 13, © Walt Disney Pictures/Photofest; 14, © Buena Vista Pictures/Everett Collection; 15, © Buena Vista Pictures/Everett Collection; 16, © Universal/ Everett Collection; 17, © Universal/Everett Collection; 18, © MGM/Photofest; 19, Courtesy Everett Collection; 20, © Courtesy of the American Humane Association; 21, © Buena Vista Pictures/ Everett Collection; 22, © Carol Rosegg; 23, Diana Walker; 24, Courtesy Everett Collection; 25, © Buena Vista Pictures/Photofest; 26, © Birds and Animals Unlimited; 27, © Birds and Animals Unlimited; 29TL, © Michael Shake/Shtterstock; 29TR, © GK Hart/Vikki Hart/Photodisc Green/ Getty Images; 29ML, © PhotoSpin; 29MR, © Alan & Sandy Carey/Photodisc Green/Getty Images; 29BL, © Dynamic Graphics Group/Creatas/Alamy; 29BR, © Image Ideas/Index Stock Imagery/ Newscom.com.

Publisher: Kenn Goin
Project Editor: Lisa Wiseman
Creative Director: Spencer Brinker
Photo Researcher: Marty Levick
Original Design: Dawn Beard Creative

Library of Congress Cataloging-in-Publication Data

Goldish, Meish.
  Hollywood dogs / by Meish Goldish.
    p. cm. — (Dog heroes)
  Includes bibliographical references and index.
  ISBN-13: 978-1-59716-404-7 (library binding)
  ISBN-10: 1-59716-404-6 (library binding)
  1. Working dogs—United States—Juvenile literature. 2. Animals in motion pictures—United States—Juvenile literature. I. Title.

  SF428.2.G65 2007
  791.4302'80929—dc22

                          2006030995

For more information, write to Bearport Publishing Company, Inc., 101 Fifth Avenue, Suite 6R, New York, New York 10003. Printed in the United States of America.

10 9 8 7 6 5 4 3 2 1

Table of Contents

Lassie to the Rescue

A blind man and his guide dog were crossing the street. Suddenly, a motorcycle hit them. They needed help! Luckily, a boy, named Timmy, and his collie, Lassie, were nearby. They rushed over. No one was badly hurt, but the guide dog was afraid to put his **harness** back on. Lassie knew just what to do. She stepped into the harness. After seeing how brave Lassie was, the guide dog put on the harness and went back to work.

Lassie and Timmy were best friends.

This story is not real. It happened on a popular television show, *Lassie*. TV viewers fell in love with this smart, brave, and caring dog. Week after week, she solved problems for her TV family and neighbors. Lassie seemed almost human!

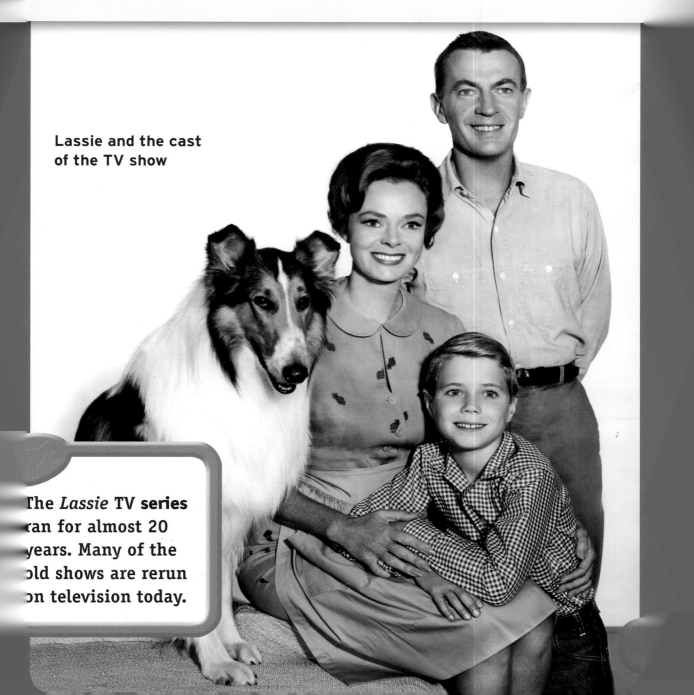

Lassie and the cast of the TV show

The *Lassie* TV **series** ran for almost 20 years. Many of the old shows are rerun on television today.

A Lucky Break

Before her TV show, Lassie starred in movies. The Hollywood career of the dog that played Lassie began with a lucky break. In 1943, a **studio** was making a film called *Lassie Come Home*. Animal trainer Rudd Weatherwax had his collie, Pal, **audition** for the lead role. Another collie won the part. However, Pal was asked to be a **stunt** dog on the movie.

Trainer Rudd Weatherwax and Lassie review a document that named Lassie honorary chairman of National Dog Week for the week of September 18, 1948.

During the filming, Lassie had to swim across a river. The dog playing Lassie refused. Weatherwax told the director that Pal could do it. Pal jumped into the water and swam across, just as he was instructed to do.

Pal became the new Lassie. The director said, "Pal went into that river, but Lassie swam out!"

The movie *Lassie Come Home* was based on a popular book by Eric Knight.

More than 300 dogs auditioned for the role of Lassie in the 1943 movie.

Star Treatment

Lassie Come Home was a big hit. Pal played the lead role in six more movies. He also starred in the first *Lassie* TV show.

Pal become a major Hollywood **celebrity**. His name was even changed to Lassie. He got thousands of fan letters a week. The studio sent out his photo with his paw print stamped on it. It was called a "pawtograph"!

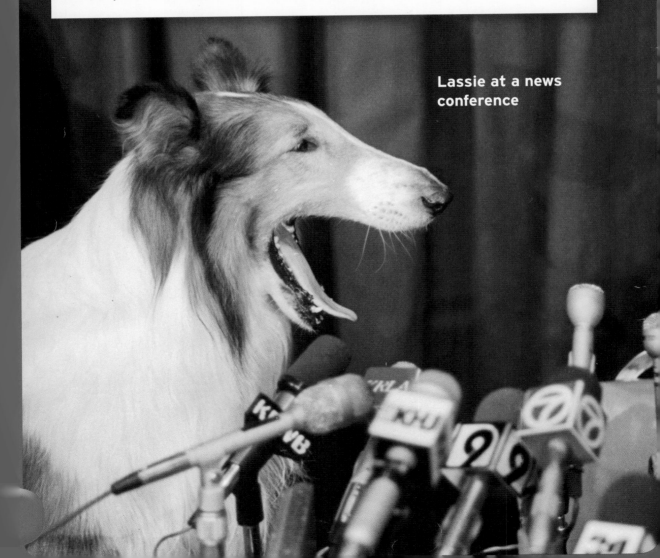

Lassie at a news conference

Lassie lived like a star, too. He slept in his own large bedroom in his trainer's home. He ate in the best restaurants and stayed in fancy hotels. Lassie had his own car, boat, and private plane. He even had his own pet dog!

Pal was a male dog who played a female role. Why? Male collies have more fur than females, so they look better on camera.

Lassie the star

From Homeless to Hollywood

Before Lassie, Hollywood already had a famous dog. He was a German shepherd named Rin-Tin-Tin. An American Army officer, Lee Duncan, found the homeless pup in France after World War I (1914–1918). He brought the **canine** home to California, where he trained "Rinty" to be a **performer**.

Rin-Tin-Tin was the first big Hollywood canine star. Unlike many others, Rin-Tin-Tin did his own action stunts.

Rin-Tin-Tin developed an amazing talent. He could leap nearly 12 feet (4 m) high. This skill got him a part in a movie in 1922 and made him famous.

During his career, Rin-Tin-Tin made more than 25 movies. He was paid $1,000 a week. At the time, most people did not earn that much money. Rin-Tin-Tin, however, was a star. He even wore a dog collar with real diamonds!

Rin-Tin-Tin movies were followed by a popular TV series in the 1950s.

Rin-Tin-Tin was named after toy puppets that were popular with children in France.

Finding Shelter

Dog stars can come from anywhere. Higgins, a mixed **breed**, was living in an animal **shelter** in California. He was rescued by Frank Inn, a dog trainer.

Higgins was a smart dog. He learned tricks quickly. In 1974, he starred in the movie *Benji*. It was a huge hit.

Movie audiences fell in love with the character of Benji.

News spread that the star had come from an animal shelter. Americans soon **adopted** more than a million dogs.

More *Benji* movies followed. When Higgins got older, the director needed a new dog to play the part. So he searched animal shelters, hoping to find another star. Fortunately, he soon found one.

After a film is made, most trainers keep the movie dogs instead of returning them to shelters.

Benji works with another animal actor in the 1987 movie *Benji the Hunted*.

Tricks of the Trade

Some movie dogs perform amazing tricks. Buddy, a golden retriever, played basketball in the movie *Air Bud* (1997). His trainer, Debra Coe, taught him how to sink baskets. It took six months and nearly 4,000 tries to make his first one. Yet practice makes perfect. Buddy made more than 20,000 baskets in his career!

Often, Buddy needed many tries to sink a basket. However, in the end, he always succeeded.

Buddy used special basketballs in *Air Bud*. They were lighter and softer than real ones. They were also covered with grease. To make a basket, the trainer threw a ball at Buddy. The dog would leap up and try to bite it. Since the ball was greasy, he wasn't able to grab it. Instead, as the ball hit his mouth he pushed it toward the basket. Score!

Buddy wore special sneakers made to fit his paws.

The special basketballs used in *Air Bud* cost about $300 each.

Behind the Scenes

Dog actors often do tricks with hidden help. The star of *Beethoven* (1992) was a Saint Bernard. In one scene, he had to drag two people who were wrapped up in his leash. The couple sat on chairs by a table. On screen, it looked as if the dog was pulling the people, chairs, and table. However, even Beethoven wasn't that strong!

The movie **crew** planned the scene carefully. They tied the table and chairs to a cable. The cable was attached to a truck. During filming, the truck stayed hidden from view as it pulled everything, including the couple. Beethoven simply ran alongside the cable. Yet it looked as if he was doing all the work.

A scene from the movie *Beethoven*

In *Beethoven's 2nd* (1993), the sequel to *Beethoven*, baby food was rubbed on Beethoven's face to get Missy (right) to kiss him.

Dog food is sometimes placed on an actor's clothes to get a dog to walk over to him or her.

Stage Fright

Most Hollywood hounds like Beethoven are lively. However, Terry, a cairn terrier, was different. She was very shy. When Carl Spitz first tried to train her, she hid under a bed for three weeks!

Later, a movie director saw Terry. He thought she was perfect for the role of Toto in the movie *The Wizard of Oz* (1939). She got the part.

The movie *The Wizard of Oz* was based on the book *The Wonderful Wizard of Oz* by L. Frank Baum.

Terry faced many challenges on the movie set. She was afraid of the large wind machines that blew during the storm scenes. Even worse, an actor accidentally stepped on her foot and **sprained** it. After several weeks, Terry recovered. She bravely finished the movie and became a star!

Terry won the movie role because she looked like the drawings of Toto in the original book.

Safety First

Years ago, animals often got hurt on movie sets. Today, the American Humane Association (AHA) works to keep the animals safe. Before a movie is made, people at the AHA read the **script**. Then they discuss scenes with the director. They also watch the actual filming to make sure the animal actors are never at risk.

An AHA worker watches a dolphin during the shooting of the 1993 film *Flipper*.

In *The Shaggy Dog* (2006), a canine had to run into a closed window. The stunt was too dangerous for a real animal. The AHA asked the director to use a fake dog's head instead. On screen, it looked real.

At the end of the movie, the AHA stated: "No animals were harmed in the making of this motion picture."

A scene from
The Shaggy Dog

The AHA prevents animal actors from working too long without taking a break.

Live on Stage

A movie scene may be filmed many times. In plays, however, there are no second chances. A dog starring on Broadway must get it right the first time.

Cindy Lou played the part of Sandy in the musical *Annie* (1997). Trainer Bill Berloni taught her how to roll over and lie on her back on **cue**. She had to learn to be still when other actors said her name. Yet when Annie said it, she had to walk over to her.

Annie and Sandy (Cindy Lou) during a performance

During **rehearsals**, Berloni used a piece of meat to help Cindy Lou learn her part. When she smelled the food, she knew where to stop on stage. Then, during the actual show, Berloni stood off stage. He gave her hand signals telling her to "stay," "sit," or "look left and right."

Before Cindy Lou became a Broadway star, she was a **stray** dog.

Like all actors, dogs must prepare before going on stage each night.

Spots in the Spotlight

Working with just one dog can be hard. Working with hundreds is a real challenge! Gary Gero had to train 230 puppies for the movie *101 Dalmatians* (1996). He needed more than 101 dogs for a good reason. Pups grow quickly. During filming, a new batch of puppies replaced the old ones every week.

Using new dogs caused a problem. Dalmatian pups do not look exactly the same. The size and placement of their spots are different. So how could pups that did not look alike play the same character?

All it took was a little help from a make-up artist. The dogs' spots were added and removed with a safe color **dye**. After filming, the dye washed off easily.

Many other animals besides Dalmatians, such as these raccoons, were trained for *101 Dalmatians*.

The person in charge of the animals in a movie is called a wrangler.

How to Become a Star

Many proud dog owners think their dogs could be Hollywood stars. Trainer Gary Gero runs an animal talent **agency**. He looks for dogs that can sit, stay, walk, and bark on command. They should be able to learn new tricks quickly, as well as fetch objects and crawl backwards. Also, they must know how to remain still in a noisy setting.

Gary Gero gives Ketch the command to bark.

Gero says dog actors must be healthy. They need lots of energy. They should look happy and excited. Like human actors, dogs must also look right for the part.

Few dogs become movie stars. It takes talent and luck to succeed. Yet one thing is certain. In the future, Hollywood hounds will continue to thrill movie audiences!

Kristy Campbell, who works with Gary Gero, trains Eddie.

Dog actors learn to perform, even with bright lights, loud noises, and busy people all around them.

Just the Facts

- After Pal retired as Lassie, his sons and grandsons continued to play the role in films and on TV.

- Some of Rin-Tin-Tin's relatives work today as real-life search-and-rescue dogs.

- A total of 40 animal trainers worked on the set of *101 Dalmatians*. The cast and crew had to wash their feet before walking through the "puppy area." It helped to keep the fragile pups safe from disease.

- The first dog to play Sandy in *Annie* on Broadway appeared in 2,333 performances.

- Often, several look-alike dogs play the same character in a movie. Each dog is used for a different job. One dog may be best for doing stunts. Another dog may look cutest in close-up shots. Another dog may be friendliest with human actors.

- About 75 percent of all dog actors come from animal shelters.

- The American Humane Association began to protect animal actors after a horse was run off a cliff and killed during the filming of a movie in 1939.

Common Breeds: Hollywood DOGS

collie

German shepherd

golden retriever

Saint Bernard

cairn terrier

Dalmatian

adopted (uh-DOPT-id) took a child or animal into one's home to become his or her legal guardian

agency (AY-juhn-see) a business that performs a service for people

audition (aw-DISH-uhn) a performance that an actor gives to see if he or she is right for a part

breed (BREED) a particular type of animal

canine (KAY-nine) a dog

celebrity (suh-LEB-ruh-tee) a famous person or animal, such as a movie star

crew (KROO) a team of people who work together

cue (KYOO) a signal to speak or move that is given in a movie or play

dye (DYE) a chemical or substance used to change the color of something

harness (HAR-niss) a device made of leather and metal that helps an owner or trainer hold on to a working animal

performer (pur-FOR-mur) someone who entertains an audience

rehearsals (ri-HURSS-uhlz) practices for a performance

script (SKRIPT) the written text of a movie, play, or TV show

series (SIHR-eez) a number of TV shows about the same characters

shelter (SHEL-tur) a place where a homeless animal can stay

sprained (SPRAYND) injured by twisting or tearing muscles

stray (STRAY) a lost cat or dog

studio (STOO-dee-oh) a company that makes movies

stunt (STUHNT) a dangerous act that takes skill and bravery to perform

Bibliography

Beck, Ken, and Jim Clark. *The Encyclopedia of TV Pets: A Complete History of Television's Greatest Animal Stars.* Nashville, TN: Rutledge Hill Press (2002).

Carroll, Willard. *I, Toto: The Autobiography of Terry, the Dog Who Was "Toto."* New York: Stewart, Tabori and Chang (2001).

Collins, Ace. *Lassie: A Dog's Life: The First Fifty Years.* New York: Penguin (1993).

Dibra, Bash, with Kitty Brown. *StarPet: How to Make Your Pet a Star.* New York: Pocket Books (2005).

Gorrell, Gena K. *Working Like a Dog: The Story of Working Dogs Through History.* Plattsburgh, NY: Tundra Books (2003).

Mehus-Roe, Kristin. *Working Dogs: True Stories of Dogs and Their Handlers.* Irvine, CA: BowTie Press (2003).

Read More

Farran, Christopher. *Dogs on the Job! True Stories of Phenomenal Dogs.* New York: Avon Books (2003).

Singer, Marilyn. *A Dog's Gotta Do What a Dog's Gotta Do.* New York: Henry Holt (2000).

Learn More Online

Visit these Web sites to learn more about Hollywood hounds:

www.airbud.com

www.benji.com

www.lassie.net

Index

About the Author

Meish Goldish has written more than 100 books for children.
He lives in Brooklyn, New York. He answers to the name Meish.